THE GOOD GRIEF JOURNAL

THE GOOD GRIEF JOURNAL

A Journey toward Healing

Jill Alexander Essbaum

Fortress Press
Minneapolis

A Companion to Good Grief

THE GOOD GRIEF JOURNAL
A Journey toward Healing

Cover Design: Brad Norr Design
Interior design: Brad Norr Design
Typesetting: PerfecType, Nashville, TN

Print ISBN: 978-1-5064-5309-5

The paper used in this publication meets the minimum requirements of American

National Standard for Information Sciences—Permanence of Paper for Printed Library Materials, ANSI Z329, 48-1984.

Manufactured in the U.S.A.

Contents

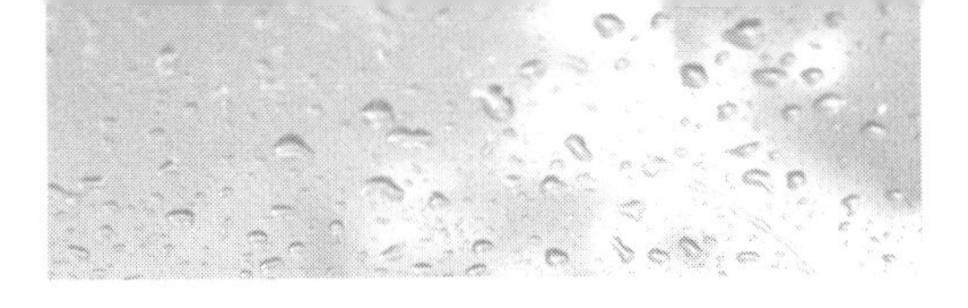

Preface

Dear Journaler:

I'd like to offer you a few wise, poignant, comforting words.

The problem is I don't have any.

And I don't have any because I'm not the expert on your grief.

You are.

You are the expert because this is your loss. These are your tears. Your sleepless nights. Your broken heart. Your prayers. Your hurt. Your healing.

And I am so, so sorry you're in pain.

What I *can* offer you, however, are the following pages on which to write your own wise, poignant, comforting words. They will be wise and comforting because you are both the author and the audience. You know what you need to say. And you know what you need to hear.

God be with you in this work.

On the Many Shapes and Sizes of Loss

Grief is a response most closely associated with physical death. Of all our losses, this one looms the largest, and it is likely that most people who pick up this journal will have done so in response to a loved one's death.

But grief does not distinguish among losses. The job you're fired from or didn't get. A looming divorce. Declining health. Bankruptcy. All losses, every one. Each deserves a fitting grief.

Even grief that follows a death will take a shape that suits the trauma of the loss. The unexpected death of a child will be felt differently from the natural passing of an elderly grandparent. A spouse is mourned one way and a parent, another. Collective grief (say, as a response to a plane crash, a natural disaster, war, or terrorism) is a shared, often public, event. By contrast, individual grief—the grief that is yours alone—is a private experience.

The meditations and prompts in this journal are intentionally nonspecific. They are adaptable to suit both the nature of your loss as well as your needs as a grieving person.

How to Use This Journal

Each of the ten meditations in this journal corresponds to a stage of grief as outlined in Granger E. Westberg's classic book *Good Grief*. Every meditation is followed by a series of prompts and questions designed to help you reflect more deeply on both the nature and effects of your loss.

Some questions are easier to answer than others. Some questions might provoke you in uncomfortable ways. I encourage you to answer them anyway. The issues that most upset us are the ones we most surely need to face.

Take your time with each prompt; speed will not serve you in this process. Write the truth as best as you know it. Grief doesn't lie to you, so do not lie to it. Do not be tempted to write what you think other people would hope to hear. This isn't a book for your spouse or your parents or your pastor. This is your journal. It's not secret, it's private. There's nothing dishonest about keeping your own thoughts close.

PREFACE

At the end of each stage you will find a page with no text. This page is also yours to use as you feel moved. Attach photos or other mementos. Draw or scribble. Write about the thoughts that seem to come to you unbidden.

Note on Verb Tense

While some stages of grief last months, others such as shock pass quickly. In fact, by the time you begin writing, you are likely to have already moved through this stage. Most of the questions in the first stage are written in the past tense. With few exceptions, present tense is used for the remaining stages. Please adjust the tenses to meet the needs of your grief work when necessary or applicable.

—Jill Alexander Essbaum

My Intentions for This Journal

Naming your intentions is a good way to begin this work, because to name a thing is to recognize its importance. Take a few moments to reflect on the following questions:

I bought this journal (or *someone gave it to me*) because

The loss I have experienced is

What I hope to work through as I write on these pages is

What I fear about this work is

If a verse of Scripture gives you comfort, courage, conviction, or all three, please copy it below.

Date ____________________

Grief

Richard Brostoff

Somewhere in the Sargasso Sea
the water disappears into itself,
hauling an ocean in.

Vortex, how you repeat
a single gesture,
come round to find only

yourself, a cup full of questions,
perhaps some curl of wisdom,
a bit of flung salt.

You hold an absence
at your center,
as if it were a life.

STAGE

1

We Are in a State of Shock

How could this have happened when everything was normal?

Joan Didion, *The Year of Magical Thinking*

The state of shock that follows any loss isn't just a kindness God affords us in the moment. It is a physical necessity. Grief demands stamina. It takes a hard toll. You endure sleepless nights and headaches born of ceaseless weeping. You eat too much. You don't eat at all. The good news is that you will heal. The bad news? *It's going to hurt.*

Shock presses pause on this process. Do not fight it. Do not fear it. Shock's an anesthetic. The numbing before the knife. It dulls a person's inconceivable agony into a temporarily bearable ache. Shock wears off but until it does, its purpose is to serve you, to still you, and to settle you down so that you may face the terrible new reality that something or someone you love is gone for good.

Consider a loss you have experienced. Did it send you into a state of shock? If so, what did the shock feel like? Did you know you were in shock as it was happening? How long did the shock last? Do you remember what it felt like to come out of it?

We Are in a State of Shock

But those who wait for the Lord
shall renew their strength,
they shall mount up with wings like eagles,
they shall run and not be weary,
they shall walk and not faint.

Isaiah 40:31

God has mercifully ordered that the human brain works slowly; first the blow, hours afterwards the bruise.

Walter de la Mare, *The Return*

Sometimes people interpret another person's state of shock as indifference and judge them accordingly. Did anyone confront you with these perceptions? How did it make you feel? How did you respond?

STAGE ONE

We Are in a State of Shock

Sometimes we interpret *our own* states of shock as indifference, and as a result, we feel both guilt and shame. Is this something you experienced? What did you say to yourself then? What would you say to yourself now?

Grief Bird

Cornelius Eady

After those buildings fell,
And New York City stank from bad intent,
And the wind twirled with human pigment,
And the sky darkened in one spot and howled,

There we walked, newborn, holding flashlights and shovels,
Dusty with shock, the streets painted mad,
Ears still smarting from the evil crumble.

Now the combing, the sifting,
Now the hauling, the uncovering.
The astonished song.

STAGE ONE

We Are in a State of Shock

Is your loss individual? Or is this a loss you share with others? Is the loss a private event or a public experience of collective suffering? Is the initial shock easier to bear alone or with others?

There is a shock that comes so quickly and strikes so deep that the blow is internalized even before the skin feels it. The strike must first reach bone marrow, then ascend slowly to the brain where the slowpoke intellect records the deed.

Maya Angelou, *Singin' and Swingin' and Gettin' Merry Like Christmas*

We Are in a State of Shock

Be still, and know that I am God.

Psalm 46:10

How, if at all, did God manifest in this stage of grief? Were you able to pray? If so, what did you pray for? Would you pray for anything different now?

We Are in a State of Shock

In the immediate aftermath of loss, friends and family often rally around to help. Were your own friends and family present for you? What did they do that was helpful? What was not helpful? Is there anything you wish someone had done?

After a great blow, or crisis, after the first shock and then after the nerves have stopped screaming and twitching, you settle down to the new condition of things and feel that all possibility of change has been used up. You adjust yourself, and are sure that the new equilibrium is for eternity. . . . But if anything is certain it is that no story is ever over, for the story which we think is over is only a chapter in a story which will not be over, and it isn't the game that is over, it is just an inning, and that game has a lot more than nine innings. When the game stops it will be called on account of darkness. But it is a long day.

Robert Penn Warren, *All the King's Men*

STAGE ONE

We Are in a State of Shock

Write a prayer invoking God's presence in the immediate aftermath of loss.

Blessed are those who mourn, for they will be comforted.

Matthew 5:4

STAGE

2

We Express Emotion

Tears are the silent language of grief.

Voltaire

The gift—and it is a gift—of shock is temporary. Numbness fades and when it does, the profound depth of your loss is no longer deniable. Then the sadness sets in. It's as real as a knife wound; your soul's been stabbed. The gears of grief begin to groan and you become a factory of tears. Days pass and it seems as if crying is the only thing you remember how to do. You feel useless. You feel used up.

But there is nothing useless about tears. Crying isn't just weeping. To cry is to call out. To cry is to express the otherwise inexpressible reality that the soul feels a pain so big and so raw that no words can accurately describe it. We should never be afraid or ashamed of expressing emotion. God made tears with a purpose in mind. God made tears that they might fall.

As a child, were you encouraged to openly express your feelings or were you taught to wall them off? Who modeled this behavior for you?

So you have pain now; but I will see you again, and your hearts will rejoice, and no one will take your joy from you.

John 16:22

We Express Emotion

Think back to your own self as a child. Who comforted you and how? If the answer is no one, then who do you wish had offered consolation? How would you have liked to have been comforted?

What was the last thing that made you cry? Where were you? What was happening? Who else was there?

STAGE TWO

We Express Emotion

Song after Sadness

Katie Ford

Despair is still servant
to the violet and wild ongoings
of bone. You, remember, are
that which must be made
servant only to salt, only
to the watery acre that is the body
of the beloved, only to the child
leaning forward into
the exhibit of birches
the forest has made of bronze light
and snow. Even as the day kneels
forward, the oceans and strung garnets, too,
kneel, they are all kneeling,
the city, the goat, the lime tree
and mother, the fearful doctor,
kneeling. Don't say it's the beautiful
I praise. I praise the human,
gutted and rising.

Mental pain is less dramatic than physical pain, but it is more common and also more hard to bear. The frequent attempt to conceal mental pain increases the burden: it is easier to say "My tooth is aching" than to say "My heart is broken."

C. S. Lewis, *The Problem of Pain*

What emotions are you experiencing right now? Are they constant, or do they change at different points throughout the day or week? Describe the experience of your shifting emotions.

STAGE TWO

We Express Emotion

My eyes waste away because of grief;
they grow weak because of all my foes.

Psalm 6:7

Do you feel comfortable expressing emotion in public? Why or why not?

STAGE TWO

We Express Emotion

At the heart of all overwhelming emotions is deep vulnerability. What makes you feel most vulnerable? What prevents you from being openly vulnerable?

He will wipe every tear from their eyes.
Death will be no more;
mourning and crying and pain will be no more,
for the first things have passed away.

Revelation 21:4

Jesus began to weep.

John 11:35

Sadness isn't the only emotion that produces tears. Joy, fear, anxiety—they all do. What other experiences cause emotion to well up in you? How do you handle those kinds of tears?

STAGE TWO

We Express Emotion

When faced with an overwhelming emotion, how do you respond?

I stood there in the shadowed doorway thinking with my tears. Yes, tears can be thoughts, why not?

Louise Erdrich, *The Round House*

May those who sow in tears
reap with shouts of joy.

Psalm 126:5

STAGE TWO

We Express Emotion

Write a prayer that asks God to help you navigate your feelings and emotions. In this prayer, freely ask of the Lord what you long for, what you need.

____

____

____

____

____

____

____

____

____

____

____

____

____

____

____

____

For everything there is a season, . . .
a time to weep, and a time to laugh;
a time to mourn, and a time to dance.

Ecclesiastes 3:1–4

STAGE

3

We Feel Depressed and Very Lonely

Loneliness got a mind of its own
The more people around the more you feel alone

Bob Dylan, "Marchin' to the City"

Loneliness follows loss like night follows sunset. It's as if grief moves in and builds an invisible, impenetrable wall between you and the rest of the world. No one can touch you, and you cannot reach out. The alienation is palpable: *you aren't just alone, you're desperately alone*. Even God is gone.

Sadness feasts on isolation. It fattens and grows into despair, which in turn reinforces just how remote you feel. How distant. How far away. Hopelessness is just around the corner. And after that? *A horizon of endless pain.*

But the pain *does* end. The black clouds dissipate. The wall between you and the world dissolves. God's absence becomes God's presence. No, you cannot click your heels or flip a switch to hurry things along. The process is deliberate. Your progress is the fruit of patience and the promise of a coming, calming peace. Therefore, watch and wait. Be vigilant and kindest to yourself. The night will fall. But mourning lifts at dawn.

Come to me, all you that are weary and are carrying heavy burdens, and I will give you rest.

Matthew 11:28

Navigating loneliness is hard. Do you have supportive people in your life? How are these people helping? How are they failing to help? Are you more likely to ask for help or to push people away? Why? Is self-protection a motivation for excluding people from your suffering? What are you protecting yourself from?

STAGE THREE

We Feel Depressed and Very Lonely

The experience of loss is deeply personal and difficult to articulate as it is happening. The inability to accurately express your sorrow further alienates you from the people in your life. Take this space to write out as complete a description of your loss as possible.

Turn to me and be gracious to me,
for I am lonely and afflicted.

Psalm 25:16

STAGE THREE

We Feel Depressed and Very Lonely

Do you think there are any spiritual or psychological benefits to loneliness? What are they? If so, how have you benefited? If not, how has loneliness harmed you either psychologically or spiritually?

People experience depression in many ways, both physical and spiritual. How does depression manifest in your life? Had you experienced depression before your loss? If so, how did it differ from what you face now?

STAGE THREE

We Feel Depressed and Very Lonely

There is no point treating a depressed person as though she were just feeling sad, saying, There now, hang on, you'll get over it. Sadness is more or less like a head cold—with patience, it passes. Depression is like cancer.

Barbara Kingsolver, *The Bean Trees*

There is an endless list of spiritualized clichés pertaining to grief. *God is in control. God has a plan. He won't give you more than you can handle. Things will get better.* Even if they're offered in the spirit of love, these condolences often feel predictably glib, almost careless. What are the least helpful things people have said to you? The most helpful? What comfort or wisdom, if any, do you find in the assurance that these sympathies *intend* to offer?

STAGE THREE

We Feel Depressed and Very Lonely

It is the Lord who goes before you. He will be with you; he will not fail you or forsake you. Do not fear or be dismayed.

Deuteronomy 31:8

When are you most lonely during the day? Where are you most lonely?

STAGE THREE

We Feel Depressed and Very Lonely

Diving

Maria Duarte

The sun is going down
as the wind runs to reach
the end of the horizon.

But the sun doesn't wait
for the wind. It goes out
like a bulb in my room.

An act of disappearance.
A magic trick perceptible
only to gulls flying over

crumbs of bread. They
are the ones that have cracked
the secret of declining:

This age where everything
is a memory and the things
never done come in dreams.

The Lord is near to the brokenhearted,
and saves the crushed in spirit.

Psalm 34:18

To feel abandoned by God in your grief and suffering is natural. Even Jesus lamented his abandonment from the cross. Do you feel abandoned by God? If so, how has this affected your faith? What do you want to say to God right now? If you are angry, then tell God. If you are suffering, then share it.

STAGE THREE

We Feel Depressed and Very Lonely

Being alone does not always mean being lonely, and solitude has a healing function. Are there times when you enjoy being alone? What are you doing during those times? Do you ever find solitude beneficial? If so, how?

In the morning, while it was still very dark, he got up and went out to a deserted place, and there he prayed.

Mark 1:35

Make a list of ways you can proactively combat your loneliness. Include a list of the people whose company you enjoy, and consider how each person might be able to help you emerge from your loneliness.

STAGE THREE

We Feel Depressed and Very Lonely

Write a prayer asking God to protect you as you grieve. Ask God to bless your loneliness and to sanctify your despair.

I will not leave you orphaned; I am coming to you.

John 14:18

STAGE

4

We May Experience Physical Symptoms of Distress

I seem to myself, as in a dream,
An accidental guest in this dreadful body.

Anna Akhmatova, ***The Complete Poems of Anna Akhmatova***

Grief takes place in bodies. It is not an abstract process you can rationalize or reason through. It's a visceral, physical event. Your suffering? It's real. And it isn't in your head. It's in your heart. You will heal, but first you must mourn, and before that can happen it is essential to acknowledge both the fact and the depth of your loss. This requires courage and consciousness.

While it's possible to momentarily dodge your grief, there are consequences. Internalized loss will always manifest as illness. The migraine that comes and goes then comes again. Throbbing joints and mysterious fevers. A nebulous ache that puts you in bed for a week. Your agony, while genuine, is untreatable by pill. The process of grieving cannot be medicated away. The grief itself is the remedy for the loss.

Beloved, I pray that all may go well with you and that you may be in good health, just as it is well with your soul.

3 John 1:2

Were you healthy before your loss? How is your health now? What, if anything, has changed?

STAGE FOUR

We May Experience Physical Symptoms of Distress

Are you concerned about your health in general?

So we do not lose heart. Even though our outer nature is wasting away, our inner nature is being renewed day by day.

2 Corinthians 4:16

Has unaddressed grief affected your health? If so, in what way?

For I will restore health to you,
and your wounds I will heal, says the Lord.

Jeremiah 30:17

STAGE FOUR

We May Experience Physical Symptoms of Distress

Taking care of yourself is always important, but after a loss, it's imperative. Do you have a self-care regime? If so, how do you nurture your body (diet, exercise, sleep, and so forth)? Have you been able to sustain these practices while grieving? If you do not take care of your body, why is that?

Loss

Rodney Gomez

Lately I have been a gap.
Moth clouds follow me to bed.
I counted them: twenty, fifty, block, choke.

In the room where I used to sleep
a breath hangs low on the bed
and hoarsens the room.
No one knows where the air is
charged and released into the world,
but it thistles.

This is how breathing fills a house
with family: breathing to draw
the buzzing to its source
and breathing to lacquer a plugged maze.

How a house fully beamed and walled
is not a house, but a husk.
How a life in the span of a few breaths
becomes a clockless thing.

STAGE FOUR

We May Experience Physical Symptoms of Distress

One day, the pain will be gone and you will still be there.

Harold Kushner, *When All You've Ever Wanted Isn't Enough*

Grief affects every aspect of well-being, including mental, emotional, and sexual health. Have you experienced problems related to these areas? What issues have you faced? What steps can you take to address any problems you may experience now or in the future?

Jesus went throughout Galilee, teaching in their synagogues and proclaiming the good news of the kingdom and curing every disease and every sickness among the people.

Matthew 4:23

STAGE FOUR

We May Experience Physical Symptoms of Distress

Write a prayer asking God to either restore or sustain your health. Ask for the specific help you need.

I can do all things through him who strengthens me.

Philippians 4:13

STAGE

5

We May Become Panicky

I'm not afraid of storms, for I'm learning how to sail my ship.

Louisa May Alcott, *Little Women*

The world is full of things to fear. Scary dogs. Prowlers in the night. So many monsters underneath so many beds. Loss will trigger terrors of its own. You tense each time the phone rings. *What or whom have I lost now?* Every line of reasoning ends in a worst-case scenario. Your thoughts race on a hamster wheel, and you spin, too, teetering on the brink of what you are certain is interminable madness.

You are not losing your mind. Fear is a rational response to the unknown, and loss strips life from all familiarity. While you may not be able to entirely avoid the anxiety of this stage of grief, remember that you don't have to rely on your own ability to overcome your fears. You might be terrified, but God is not afraid. His is not the spirit of fear, but of love and power and a whole, sound mind. No, you are not insane. You are in grief.

What are you afraid of? List everything that comes to mind, even if it seems small or insignificant. What about these things frightens you?

We May Become Panicky

Be strong and bold; have no fear or dread of them, because it is the Lord your God who goes with you; he will not fail you or forsake you.

Deuteronomy 31:6

It is a strange thing, but when you are dreading something, and would give anything to slow down time, it has a disobliging habit of speeding up.

J. K. Rowling, *Harry Potter and the Goblet of Fire*

Do you ever feel like you are spinning out of control? What initiates this feeling? How do you calm yourself down?

STAGE FIVE

We May Become Panicky

4:13 am

Jill Alexander Essbaum

The shift of sleepwalks and suicides.
The occasion of owls and a demi-lune fog.
Even God has nodded off

And won't be taking prayers til ten.
Ad interim, you put them on.
As if your wants could keep you warm.

As if. You say your shibboleths.
You thumb your beads. You scry the glass.
Night creeps to its precipice

And the broken rim of reason breaks
Again. An obsidian sky betrays you.
Every serrate shadow flays you.

Soon enough, the crow will caw.
The cock will crow. The door will close.
(*He isn't coming back, you know.*)

And so wee, wet hours of grief relent.
In thirty years you might forget
Precisely how tonight's pain felt.

And in whose black house you dwelt.

Panic clouds both thinking and judgment. Making a list of self-soothing strategies that you can rely on when panic strikes is both useful and pragmatic. What are some things that you can remind yourself to do when anxiety and fear overcome you?

STAGE FIVE

We May Become Panicky

The ability to distract one's self from panic is one example of a useful strategy for managing anxiety. Humor, work, and exercise are a few possible distractions. Make your own list of possible distractions.

When the cares of my heart are many,
your consolations cheer my soul.

Psalm 94:19

But now thus says the Lord,
he who created you, O Jacob,
he who formed you, O Israel:
Do not fear, for I have redeemed you;
I have called you by name, you are mine.

Isaiah 43:1

What would a day without anxiety or panic look like to you?

STAGE FIVE

We May Become Panicky

For I am convinced that neither death, nor life, nor angels, nor rulers, nor things present, nor things to come, nor powers, nor height, nor depth, nor anything else in all creation, will be able to separate us from the love of God in Christ Jesus our Lord.

Romans 8:38–39

I sought the Lord, and he answered me,
and delivered me from all my fears.

Psalm 34:4

Prepare one or two short affirmations ("I am well" or "This is a panic attack; I am not in danger") that you can say to yourself when panic arises. Write something that is easy to memorize.

STAGE FIVE

We May Become Panicky

Write a prayer asking God to be present in all times of fear and anxiety.

Peace I leave with you; my peace I give to you. I do not give to you as the world gives. Do not let your hearts be troubled, and do not let them be afraid.

John 14:27

STAGE

6

We Feel a Sense of Guilt about the Loss

Guilt is perhaps the most painful companion of death.

Elisabeth Kübler-Ross, *On Death and Dying*

Guilt can grind your grieving to a halt. At its best, guilt is the conscience's way of helping reconcile actions to consequences. Appropriate guilt precedes forgiveness by instructing us in the ways of accountability, contrition, and grace.

At its worst, guilt is a paralytic. Neurotic guilt is unwarranted guilt. It attacks logic and contorts reality. This kind of guilt incriminates you into believing you are responsible for things over which you have no control. Every action feels erroneous. Apologizing for your existence becomes your life's work.

Overcoming neurotic guilt requires tremendous patience and the ability to be unflinchingly rational. Ask yourself: *Is this an instance in which I am truly culpable? Have I legitimately committed an offense?* If the answer is no, then you must accept it, if not willingly, then resolutely, trusting in the Lord to give you the wisdom you prayerfully and sincerely seek to discern.

Do you feel guilt in relation to your loss? If so, what is the source of this guilt?

STAGE SIX

We Feel a Sense of Guilt about the Loss

In all of our lives, there are days that we wish we could see expunged from the record of our very existence. Perhaps we long for that erasure because a particular day brought us such splintering sorrow that we can scarcely bear to think of it ever again. Or we might wish to blot out an episode forever because we behaved so poorly on that day—we were mortifyingly selfish, or foolish to an extraordinary degree. Or perhaps we injured another person and wish to disremember our guilt. Tragically, there are some days in a lifetime when all three of those things happen at once—when we are heartbroken and foolish and unforgivably injurious to others, all at the same time.

Elizabeth Gilbert, *The Signature of All Things*

Is this legitimate or neurotic guilt? Can you tell the difference? If you cannot, do you have a trusted friend you can consult? How would you frame your question to this friend?

Put on the whole armor of God, so that you may be able to stand against the wiles of the devil.

Ephesians 6:11

STAGE SIX

We Feel a Sense of Guilt about the Loss

If your guilt has a legitimate basis, is there anything you can do to make restitution? Are you able to ask for forgiveness? What else might you do to resolve this sense of guilt?

What could you have controlled in this situation? What was beyond your control?

STAGE SIX

We Feel a Sense of Guilt about the Loss

If it's not possible to ask for forgiveness in person, ask for forgiveness here, in writing.

Search me, O God, and know my heart;
test me and know my thoughts.
See if there is any wicked way in me,
and lead me in the way everlasting.

Psalm 139:23–24

Even the Dead Do It

Sue Owen

Feel regret about the one
event that led them there,
the cough that cracked the rib,
the ladder rung that broke

the neck, or the knife that
plunged too deep into the heart.
It's all a matter of perspective,
the dead think, as they lie

in that underground darkness.
It's all a matter of the silence
of eternity, as no breath
ever comes back for a short

visit, even for old time's sake.
And since the dead can't talk,
what else is there to do
but to think hard about the pain

STAGE SIX

We Feel a Sense of Guilt about the Loss

and brevity of their lives,
the lost chances and wrong turns?
But even that could lead
to many headaches and the old

insomnia, when death was
billed as peaceful, even serene.
So why trouble with the thinking,
after all, the dead think?

All that is required of us in
this cemetery is what our bones
politely arranged, what the
prayer meant as the coffin shut.

Many religious denominations include, in their liturgies, sacraments of confession and absolution, which can be performed privately or in a group. Is this something you would find helpful? If so, what do you need to do to participate in such a ritual?

STAGE SIX

We Feel a Sense of Guilt about the Loss

Do you believe that God forgives all who ask? Do you believe God forgives you?

If we confess our sins, he who is faithful and just will forgive us our sins and cleanse us from all unrighteousness.

1 John 1:9

Is it difficult for you to forgive others? If a friend approached you with earnest regret and guilt, how would you respond?

STAGE SIX

We Feel a Sense of Guilt about the Loss

Write a prayer asking God to help you learn to recognize appropriate guilt as well as to reject neurotic guilt. Ask for the forgiveness you desire.

So if anyone is in Christ, there is a new creation: everything old has passed away; see, everything has become new!

2 Corinthians 5:17

STAGE

7

We Are Filled with Anger and Resentment

This was a little house, with a ceiling that kept getting higher and higher, a hot place with no windows. This was anger.

Helen Oyeyemi, *The Icarus Girl*

Imagine a backpack filled with bricks. Imagine that you wear it day and night for weeks or months or years. While showering. At work. In bed. You never take it off.

Anger is a natural reaction to deep loss. It isn't wrong; some griefs *demand* our screams.

And anger has a knack for motivating change. No spiritual failure here. Even Jesus blew his top.

But anger lugged around too long will knock you out. Like that brick-filled bag, old angers curve your spine and pain your gait. They'll break your neck.

Anger resolution is a slow, hard chore. But you won't pass through grief until it's done. Remove the backpack. Take the bricks. Begin to build your life again.

What triggers your anger?

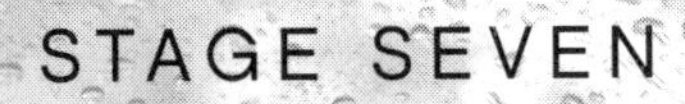

We Are Filled with Anger and Resentment

Do you have strategies for controlling outbursts of anger? If so, what are they? If not, then prepare a list of possible strategies.

Put away from you all bitterness and wrath and anger and wrangling and slander, together with all malice.

Ephesians 4:31

STAGE SEVEN

We Are Filled with Anger and Resentment

We learn in childhood how to manage our anger as adults. How did the adults in your life (parents, grandparents, teachers) manage their anger, if at all? Did they respond to your anger with patience, or did they dismiss your feelings as immature or unwarranted? How has this influenced your ability to manage anger now?

Loss gives you the right to be angry—with a person, an event, an institution, even God. Speak to the source of your anger. Do not hold back.

STAGE SEVEN

We Are Filled with Anger and Resentment

Be angry but do not sin; do not let the sun go down on your anger.

Ephesians 4:26

Bittersweet

Rhina Espaillat

My friend—that best of gardeners—pulls out
green yards and yards of tentacles whose tight
coils twine through my roses, feel about
for the next host to strangle. And she's right,
of course; there's nothing lovable in this
opportunistic scrambler for the sun
that flatters as it kills, each Judas kiss
of berry fat with seeds, a loaded gun
of generation. Still, there's something true
in aims so narrow that they leave no room
for reason. What these climbers do, they do
heeding that first imperative: to bloom.
One could, if one were mastered by rank joy,
shield what a better gardener would destroy.

STAGE SEVEN

We Are Filled with Anger and Resentment

Are you angry at yourself? If so, why?

Many people turn to the creative arts to express strong feelings. Write a poem about your anger. Draw a picture representing your anger.

STAGE SEVEN

We Are Filled with Anger and Resentment

A positive aspect of anger is that it contains a great deal of energy. Angry energy can be constructive, spurring either personal or societal change for good (for example, John Walsh creating the television series *America's Most Wanted* after the murder of his son or the Black Lives Matter movement, which grew as a response to racial violence). Is it possible to use your anger to enact positive change in either your own life or in the lives of others? How can you make this happen? List the specific steps that you must take to make constructive and creative use of your anger.

STAGE SEVEN

We Are Filled with Anger and Resentment

I couldn't write it in anger. . . . I need all of my skills, all of the control, all of my powers, and I need clarity in order to write.

Toni Morrison, on her novel *Beloved*, interview with CBS Radio host Don Swaim, October 26, 1987

Refrain from anger, and forsake wrath.
Do not fret—it leads only to evil.

Psalm 37:8

How does anger affect your relationships? How does it affect your emotional life?

We Are Filled with Anger and Resentment

Write a prayer asking God for guidance in controlling and, ultimately, releasing your anger.

By contrast, the fruit of the Spirit is love, joy, peace, patience, kindness, generosity, faithfulness, gentleness, and self-control. There is no law against such things.

Galatians 5:22–23

STAGE

8

We Resist Returning

I am beginning to see that much of praying is grieving.

Henri Nouwen, *Return of the Prodigal Son*

Grief doesn't run on a timetable. It's not a scheduled event. You can't set your watch alarm by its stages or count down days on the calendar until you reach the end of your suffering. How long does it take to grieve? *It takes as long as it takes.*

You might be tempted to retreat into your grief. You've lived with it a long time. It's a known quantity and an intimate companion. This familiarity carries a paradoxical comfort. However unpleasant your feelings are, they are feelings you recognize. You have been acclimated to a new normal. You might also worry that your grief is incomplete or even inadequate. Your reluctance to return may be compounded by worries stemming from the character or the duration of your grief. *Have I sufficiently mourned? Was I sad enough?* Friend, these are qualities that cannot be measured.

It's true: life after loss is terrifying. But the length of your grief isn't what honors the depth of your pain. A good grief helps you survive your loss. Search your heart. You'll know when it's time to move forward. The land of the living awaits you.

Are there situations, places, or people you find yourself avoiding? Are they connected with your loss? What makes you want to avoid them? What would happen if you didn't avoid them?

STAGE EIGHT

We Resist Returning

Trust in the Lord with all your heart,
and do not rely on your own insight.
In all your ways acknowledge him,
and he will make straight your paths.

Proverbs 3:5–6

Are you afraid of not grieving enough? What, in your mind, would constitute grieving enough?

You never depart from us, but yet, only with difficulties do we return to You.

Augustine of Hippo, *Confessions*

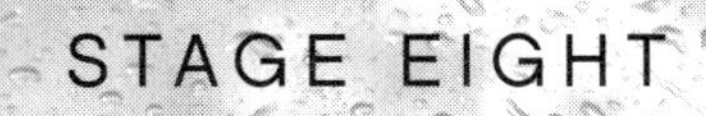

STAGE EIGHT

We Resist Returning

As you're trying to regain your foothold on life, it's helpful to have a plan of action. Take this space to come up with a daily list of things to do to help you step back into the world. Try and make it as specific as possible. Don't judge yourself. "Get dressed" and "brush teeth" are acceptable tasks to put on your checklist.

While it's crucial to have a support network throughout all stages of grief, it's especially important to have one as you navigate your post-loss life. Make a list of the people you can turn to for help. Include specific ways that each person can support you *(cooking, meeting over coffee, taking a walk, picking up children from school)*.

STAGE EIGHT

We Resist Returning

Bliss

Jessica Piazza

is the last
thing you miss

when your fortune
has circled

and the fetters
that formerly

thwarted you
lift. Like a whelk

unmoored, you
still shore safely

and unscathed
inside your shell.

Unsure if it's
a heaven or a hell.

Beloved, I do not consider that I have made it my own; but this one thing I do: forgetting what lies behind and straining forward to what lies ahead, I press on toward the goal for the prize of the heavenly call of God in Christ Jesus.

Philippians 3:13–14

Engaging in pleasurable activities can help smooth the transition as you return from grief. What do you enjoy? Is there an activity you've always wanted to try but haven't yet? If so, what stops you from trying it? Use this space to make concrete plans to try something new.

STAGE EIGHT

We Resist Returning

Write a prayer asking God's blessing on you as you return to your daily activities. Ask for guidance in rebuilding your life, and wisdom in moving forward.

____

____

____

____

____

____

____

____

____

____

____

____

____

Do not remember the former things,
or consider the things of old.
I am about to do a new thing;
now it springs forth, do you not perceive it?
I will make a way in the wilderness
and rivers in the desert.

Isaiah 43:18–19

STAGE

9

Gradually Hope Comes Through

There is a crack, a crack in everything.
That's how the light gets in.

Leonard Cohen, "Anthem"

It's hard to speak of hope without lapsing into platitudes. How it springs eternal. That shiny silver linings are quilted into clouds. All those everythings that happen for a reason. These glib and threadbare sound bites do little good. They insult the profound nature of grief.

Real hope is anything but ordinary. Hope's heart beats with possibility. Hope makes plans. Hope has the capacity for pleasure and delight. Hope is the forerunner to joy. Hope's message is unambiguous: *your loss does not define you.*

At the onset of grief, it's impossible and frankly counterproductive to imagine a future that exists beyond it. Hope grows slowly. Watching its pot won't make it boil. Spend your energies on the grieving process. Each step prepares you for the next. You're not waiting on hope. Hope is waiting on you.

I feel hopeful when I . . . *(write down everything that comes to mind)*.

STAGE NINE

Gradually Hope Comes Through

May the God of hope fill you with all joy and peace in believing, so that you may abound in hope by the power of the Holy Spirit.

Romans 15:13

A Dead Thing That, in Dying, Feeds the Living

Donika Kelly

I've been thinking about the anatomy
of the egg, about the two interior membranes,

the yolk held in place by the chalazae, gases
moving through the semipermeable shell.

A curious phrase, *the anatomy of the egg,*
as if an egg were a body, which it is,

as if the egg could be broken then mended,
which, depending on your faith, broken yes,

but mended? Well. Best to start
again, with a new body, voided

from a warmer one, brooded and turned.
Better to begin as if some small-handed

animal hadn't knocked you against a rock,
licked clean the rich yolk and left

Gradually Hope Comes Through

the albumen to dry in the sun—as if a hinged
jaw hadn't swallowed you whole.

What I wanted: a practice that reassured
that what was cracked could be mended

or, at least, suspended so that it could not spread.
But now I wonder: better to be the egg or scaled

mandible? The small hand or the flies, bottle black
and green, spilling their bile onto whatever's left,

sweeping the interior, drinking it clean?
I think, *something might have grown there*, though

I know it was always meant to be eaten,
it was always meant to spoil.

Hope is that thing inside us that insists, despite all the evidence to the contrary, that something better awaits us if we have the courage to reach for it and to work for it and to fight for it.

President Barack Obama, speech after the Iowa Caucuses, January 3, 2008

When we are able to hope, we are able to see a day beyond today. This means we can start to plan for the future, both near and distant. Do you have a plan for your life? Where do you want to be a year from now? What concrete steps do you need to take to get there?

STAGE NINE

Gradually Hope Comes Through

Nothing is hopeless; we must hope for everything.

Madeleine L'Engle, *A Wrinkle in Time*

The moment we start to hope is also often the moment we start to doubt. We do not trust the hope we have. It's important to be conscious of these doubts, because we cannot overcome what we don't know. What doubts begin to surface once you have hope? Why do you think they surface? How do you address these doubts?

STAGE NINE

Gradually Hope Comes Through

Hope is a Christian virtue. How does hope manifest itself in your spiritual life? How does your post-loss hope differ from your pre-loss hope?

We also boast in our sufferings, knowing that suffering produces endurance, and endurance produces character, and character produces hope, and hope does not disappoint us, because God's love has been poured into our hearts through the Holy Spirit that has been given to us.

Romans 5:3–5

Now faith is the assurance of things hoped for, the conviction of things not seen.

Hebrews 11:1

What stands in the way of your hope?

STAGE NINE

Gradually Hope Comes Through

Personal strengths can be channeled into hope. What are your strengths?

Be strong, and let your heart take courage,
all you who wait for the Lord.

Psalm 31:24

What do you hope for in the next six months? In a year? In five years?

STAGE NINE

Gradually Hope Comes Through

Write a prayer asking God to nurture hope in you.

For surely I know the plans I have for you, says the Lord, plans for your welfare and not for harm, to give you a future with hope.

Jeremiah 29:11

STAGE

10

We Struggle to Affirm Reality

Life must be understood backwards.
But . . . it must be lived forwards.

Søren Kierkegaard, *Journals*

Jacob makes no bones about it: *I will not let you go until you bless me.* This he says to the angel he has the audacity to wrestle. And the angel indeed blesses him. But the angel wounds him too.

Grief is the byproduct of wrestling with loss. The struggle is real. You pin it to the mat; it slips from your hold. Your job is to keep wrestling. The blessing's this: *your broken heart will heal.*

But the healing will leave a scar.

We only truly mourn what we truly love. That's the wound.

So you return to your life a different person. Be gentle with yourself. Be patient. Honor your loss by making peace with it.

Grief is a tangible, undeniable fact. But so is the love of God.

The faith that sustains you through trauma is the faith that will carry you beyond it.

How has your grief changed you? Are the changes positive? How are you different from the way you were before your loss?

STAGE TEN

We Struggle to Affirm Reality

But Jesus looked at them and said, "For mortals it is impossible, but for God all things are possible."

Matthew 19:26

What brings you joy?

STAGE TEN

We Struggle to Affirm Reality

Remember that hope is a good thing, . . . maybe the best of things, and no good thing ever dies.

Stephen King, *Rita Hayworth and Shawshank Redemption*

How will you honor your loss?

Grief occasionally returns. It may return on the anniversary of your loss (sometimes even years later). It may also surface when you are under stress. When grief returns, how will you respond? What strategies might you put in place to cope with "rebound grief"?

STAGE TEN

We Struggle to Affirm Reality

Life will break you. Nobody can protect you from that, and living alone won't either, for solitude will also break you with its yearning. You have to love. You have to feel. It is the reason you are here on earth. You are here to risk your heart. You are here to be swallowed up. And when it happens that you are broken, or betrayed, or left, or hurt, or death brushes near, let yourself sit by an apple tree and listen to the apples falling all around you in heaps, wasting their sweetness. Tell yourself that you tasted as many as you could.

Louise Erdrich, *The Painted Drum*

Transformation gives us the audacity to advance along a road of unknowing.

Stanley Hauerwas, *Living Gently in a Violent World*

Define yourself. Who are you?

STAGE TEN

We Struggle to Affirm Reality

Permeable Divide

Ellen Rachlin

We are together in a galaxy called Loss.
Because I know nothing other than time and place
and where to go to speak with you,
I invented one for you.
No light, no atmosphere needed
to be who you once were.

Since there's no fooling grief,
and remembering is also what I do,
forcing thought to etch you into sight,
there is no time, no nothing—
just spaces collapsed into immortality.

Has this been a good grief? Have certain steps been more difficult than others? If so, which ones? What made these steps challenging?

The human mind plans the way,
but the Lord directs the steps.

Proverbs 16:9

We Struggle to Affirm Reality

What have you learned about yourself? What truths have you discovered through the process? In what ways will you integrate this knowledge into your daily life?

Beloved, we are God's children now; what we will be has not yet been revealed. What we do know is this: when he is revealed, we will be like him, for we will see him as he is.

1 John 3:2

What are you grateful for? Is there a blessing in your wound? If so, what is it?

STAGE TEN

We Struggle to Affirm Reality

Write a prayer asking God to sustain you in your life after loss.

Now may the Lord of peace himself give you peace at all times in all ways.

2 Thessalonians 3:16